The Vanishing New Jersey Landscape

THE VANISHING NEW JERSEY LANDSCAPE

Clem Fiori

RUTGERS UNIVERSITY PRESS • NEW BRUNSWICK, NEW JERSEY

Library of Congress Cataloging-in-Publication Data

Fiori, Clem, 1943–
   The vanishing New Jersey landscape / Clem Fiori.
      p.   cm.
   ISBN 0-8135-2091-6
   1. New Jersey—Pictorial works.   2. Landscape—New Jersey—
Pictorial works.   3. Natural areas—New Jersey.   I. Title.
F135.F55   1994
917.4904'43—dc20   93-43531
                                                CIP

British Cataloging-in-Publication information available

Frontispiece: Rosemont-Ringoes Road, looking west, Delaware Township, October 1992

This book was published with the help of the Delaware River Mill
Society and a grant from the Geraldine R. Dodge Foundation.

For my sons, Nicholas and Daniel

PREFACE

The photographs in this book are of rural places in central New Jersey, primarily in Somerset and Hunterdon counties. Most of them were made between the late summer of 1985 and early spring of 1993, although some of the pictures in the hedgerow series date back as far as 1977. The writings, which run throughout, are sometimes remembrances of my childhood, and sometimes reflections or anecdotes from more recent times relating to my experiences in making these pictures, or to my involvement as a local public official concerned with open space planning and conservation.

Other relevant facts are that I am fifty years old as I present this book to the publisher, and I have lived in Somerset County all my life. I grew up in Warren Township and lived there through my college years at Rutgers. Since then I have lived in Rocky Hill and now Blawenburg, in Montgomery Township. Over these years, and especially during the last decade, I have become acutely aware of how strong a sense of place has always been in me. The sights, sounds, smells of this countryside—the texture and color of the shale-rich soil, the typical configuration of trees as they group together in hedgerows, the jutting outcroppings of layered rock which form ridges of geologic history, the eccentrically meandering tributary streams—these all have left a lasting imprint on my mind and senses. As my life here continues to reinforce the pattern of this imprint, I experience a predictable sequence of moods directly linked to the evolving cycle of seasons, and as a gardener, cyclist, photographer, and conservationist, I fortify this link even further by spending as much time as I can out on the land.

But there are fewer open places out there these days. The arc of my personal weather vane has not so wide a circumference in which to turn. For me, and the others I talk to who share my sensitivities, there is an awareness of a critical breach of the boundaries of space around us and a compression of the medium in which we have always hoped to thrive. The frenzied land development boom experienced in this region in the 1980s has, by its explosive force, fragmented much of the countryside,

and the fissures which radiate through the few seemingly less affected areas signal the direction of future waves of encroachment. And it is not just the open land we are losing. Much of the cultural heritage represented by this landscape—the way we once knew how to occupy and utilize the open land—is also being ruthlessly obliterated. Traditionally clustered rural communities and crossroads villages, with their religious, cultural, and economic focal points, have been thoughtlessly sacrificed in deference to expedient and all-encompassing sprawls of vast tract subdivisions, which offer no sense of community, have no sensitivity to the unique geography of the region, and which monopolize as well as negatively impact all the natural resources.

As a conservationist involved in local open space planning, I am dedicated to doing what I can to revise the sense of priorities of those around me regarding what is happening right here. Often, environmental efforts tend to focus on the more vast global concerns, emphasizing threats to oceans, far-off rain forests, exotic endangered species, the ozone layer, and the like. Yet critical issues that directly affect the local watershed environments where we actually live are either summarily ignored or entrusted to the standards of municipal land use regulations, which don't take into account most of the newly emerging environmental crises and the measures that may be necessary to mitigate them.

As an artist, I must tell you that the places you see in these photographs are remnants of a region whose character is being inevitably and irreversibly transformed. Most of my childhood haunts, referred to in the text of this book, had already disappeared in this transformation process before I even started making the book. The pictures of places in Montgomery and elsewhere which remind me of these former scenes are surrogates from another time, and even many of these more contemporary views have vanished as the book was made. And so, like passing youth, the pictures and stories of these places become metaphors for all the things we cannot keep or hold.

ACKNOWLEDGMENTS

The Geraldine R. Dodge Foundation is responsible for providing the major portion of funds necessary to produce this book, and I am deeply grateful. I am especially grateful for the encouragement and spiritual support of Scott McVay, the foundation's executive director. His vocal appreciations and insights have recharged my energies on many occasions.

Jim Amon, president of the Delaware River Mill Society and executive director of the Delaware and Raritan Canal Commission, has played a key role in helping this book happen. I thank him for this, as well as for the many other ways in which he has advised and guided me in my fledgling efforts in land preservation.

Ingrid Reed, as Assistant Dean of the Woodrow Wilson School at Princeton University, was responsible for hosting the first exhibit of the early work at the university in 1986. Jamie Sapoch of the Stony Brook–Millstone Watershed Association, and Sam Hammil of M.S.M. Regional Study Council, also contributed to this first exhibit, and the Princeton Friends of Open Space were generous supporters. This early exposure generated valuable momentum and public awareness of the project, and I will never forget how important these people have been to me.

Margaret O'Reilly and Mary Penny conspired to bring about the production of a stunning little catalog of selected works to accompany the 1991 exhibit at the New Jersey Museum of Agriculture at Cook College, Rutgers. Their freely given efforts, using a grant from the Fund for New Jersey to cover printing costs, with Jamie Sapoch as coordinator, resulted in the best vehicle for communicating the work, short of this book.

Virginia Wageman, a dear personal friend for over twenty years who has helped me in my career in many significant ways, is once again responsible for getting me in the right place at the right time. Once again, I love her.

My mother and father, Grace and Lou Fiori, have always given me unqualified support for everything I ever did. This project is no exception. Thank you both for the truck, and the aerial platform, and your confidence and love. I deeply regret not having finished soon enough for Dad to have been able to see the finished book.

Joanna, my wife and the only person I totally love and completely trust, deserves more thanks than I can give her. I can't do anything without her help, and she is the most generous person in the world.

The Vanishing New Jersey Landscape

Central New Jersey agricultural landscape, in the pockets where it tenuously still exists, gives a view where the natural elements of the countryside are laid out in a distinctively revealing way. The selective clearing and sometimes terracing of upland areas allows fences, stone walls, and naturally occurring hedgerows to outline and ornament the underlying elemental design. The contours created by the plow and disc, and the later appearance of the rows of crop seedlings, give texture and movement to the earthly flesh, the soil. Rank grasses edging marshy swales and dark vulval stream cuts overhung and veiled by brambles, trees, and vines proclaim the mysteries of the breeding source within.

1. ROSEMONT–RINGOES ROAD
looking west
Delaware Township
October 1992

2. GREAT ROAD NEAR BLAWENBURG
looking southeast
Montgomery Township
September 1985

Opposite
3. NEAR FAIRVIEW ROAD
looking north
Montgomery Township
October 1985

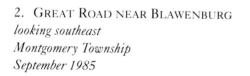

4. DUNKARD CHURCH ROAD
looking south
Delaware Township
October 1992

Opposite
5. WERTSVILLE ROAD
looking east
East Amwell Township
October 1992

6. SYCAMORE NEAR WASHINGTON WELL FARM
Route 518
Montgomery Township
April 1988

At the time I began to commit myself to photographing these rural views, I was also doing photographic work for a book project for the Princeton University Art Museum. The book was called *Images of the Mind*, and I was photographing Chinese scroll paintings of landscapes. These formal and elaborately composed paintings were idealized mind's-eye views where near, middle, and far details were combined in elegant layers, a kind of composition that could be approximated in reality only by viewing a scene from the perspective of a hilltop, treetop, tower, or some other elevated structure.

I thought that if I could achieve such a perspective with my cameras I could experience at least some of the artistic freedom of these mind painters and add layered dimensions to my compositions not possible from ground level.

It took several years for me to settle on an affordable method of doing this. To outfit myself with the conventional type of bucket rig used by utilities or cable television companies would have cost me anywhere from thirty to sixty thousand dollars; besides, the bucket would have been too small to set up a view camera on a tripod. The eventual solution proved to be right at hand. A telescoping platform rig, just like the one I had used at the museum many times to photograph floor mosaics and delicate tapestries that could not be hung, could be economically and safely mounted in the back of a pickup truck. It would easily support and accommodate both me and my view cameras at an eye-level of twenty-five feet off the ground.

*T*he high camera angle from the aerial platform makes layered compositions possible, where near, middle, and far details can be combined. Also, the high angle reveals otherwise hidden details, things impossible to see from ground level: the curves of a meandering stream, gully, or hedgerow; the true form of a shadow as it imitates a tree or the contour of a slope; the curving courses of the older roads as they were originally determined by the interlocking property lines of the early farms, the necessities of geology, or the less invasive engineering practices of rural road alignment of the past. These details can be rendered, not in the flat diagrammatic way of true aerial photographs, but in a way that preserves the immediacy of actual personal experience—like when one just crests a hillock and happens upon a view.

7. PROVINCE LINE ROAD
looking southeast
Hopewell Township
September 1988

Rigging the lift is always a chore. In the beginning it was a contest to see if it could be done at all; set the brake and flashers, mark the road with reflectors and cones, lock the platform in the up position, load the cameras, film, and other equipment onto the platform, pump the hydraulic cylinder to raise the platform, and then climb up the ladder to see if the position and elevation are correct. For this picture the truck had to be moved several times and the elevation corrected. After composing the picture, it was a matter of waiting for wind, moving clouds, and the changing light.

It was during this part, the waiting, that the security vehicle came up to where I was parked. They wanted to know, was I photographing the factory behind me and across the road?

The hedgerows that run through New Jersey countryside—where it still exists—have always evoked special moods in me. Depending on the season and the weather on a particular day, or what state of consciousness I am in, I notice and respond to these isolated rows of trees silhouetted against the sky. My favorite mood is created by the brooding and somber presence of hedgerows in early spring, when the bark is wet and darkened by the rain and the sky is balmy and gray. Buds are either just about to burst, or new leaves are still tiny enough not to obscure the gesturing shapes of trunks and branches.

These hedgerows flow along like a procession, showing movement through and along the countryside. Individual trees, bent with wind or age, intertwine limbs in supplication with neighbors, suggesting a dependence on, or connection to a greater whole. Or perhaps they symbolize individuals united by a common cause, like peace or civil rights marchers, or worshippers affirming faith by reenacting the procession up the slope of some calvary.

11. HEDGEROW
Franklin Township
March 1990

12. HEDGEROW
Montgomery Township
April 1977

*M*y most important childhood hedgerow was all sassafras. Scratching the exposed roots yielded the rich smell of root beer that all kids instantly recognize. In that hedgerow, right outside my house, we climbed the trees, captured bird's nests, built forts, and fought many mud wars.

Years later, when I was nearly forty, the trees were all standing dead. While my dad watched, I cut them down for firewood. I was shocked to learn how easy it was to fell these tall memories. The wood was so light it gave no resistance to the saw. There was hardly time to savor the aroma of the flying chips or the sweet smoke as they burned in the fireplace. The wood burned only a little longer than the newspaper used to start the fire and the warmth of the blaze quickly faded.

13. HEDGEROW
Montgomery Township
April 1977

Overleaf
14, 15. HEDGEROW
Franklin Township
April 1977

*I*n each picture, right in the center, is a dot. It marks the point where the leaves of the shutter first opened, and, instantly, where they joined back together again.

That colorless, lingering dot burns back into my mind each time I look at my photographs. It is a point in time—a still point—where I was once alive, in a place, under a sky, facing a direction, hoping, believing, and needing to feel whole.

Younger, before I photographed, I tried to move quietly: walking or running without breaking a single twig, crouching low and making a curve in my trail to keep the wind at my face.

Sometimes I would emerge from a hedgerow upon a wonderfully staged scene: wild animals exposed and unafraid in fields bordered by woods and thickets, other hedgerows, and the sky.

Many times there was nothing except me, my heart quick and expectant: just that moment with me alive, looking out.

16. HEDGEROW
Montgomery Township
April 1977

17. HEDGEROW
Montgomery Township
April 1977

18. HEDGEROW
Montgomery Township
April 1977

19. JOHN DRAKE ON THE TRACTOR
Route 518 near Route 206
looking south
Montgomery Township
April 1991

20. HEDGEROW NEAR
MOUNTAIN VIEW ROAD
Montgomery Township
April 1990

*H*ere is a short version of how my family got to be country folk and I got to be born and grow up in rural Warren, Somerset County, New Jersey.

At some time just prior to World War II, an eight-acre lot had been parcelled out of the surrounding farmland in the Washington Valley area of the township, and on this piece existed a small farmhouse on a stone rubble foundation, originally built soon after the end of the Civil War. The house stood close to the valley road, with a barn and coops to one side, and the whole eight acres of the newly created lot made a long rectangle two acres wide and four acres deep.

My aunt Elvira and her cousin Joe were driving by and spotted it for sale. She was in the process of trying to hatch some variation on the theme of the great American dream. The particulars differ among family members, but generally the plan involved entrepreneurial schemes ranging from agricultural pursuits, most prominently one of raising squabs for sale to restaurants, to non-agricultural schemes such as subdividing farmland into building lots and selling them, along with architectural plans, for development. These schemes, over time, would involve the participation of a number of her nine brothers and sisters, along with their spouses where they existed, plus her parents—my maternal grandparents—Mamie and Mario.

The family had lived just about everywhere: Boston, where Mario and Mamie, recently arrived from Sicily, were married; Westville, New Haven, and Wallingford, Connecticut; Mott Street in Manhattan; Williams-burg, Brooklyn; the Corona section of Queens; Sunnyside, and then finally out on Greenpoint Avenue. As head of the family, Mario had launched himself in many different directions as fish salesman, custom shoemaker, saloonkeeper, factory worker, and even undertaker. Overall, he had a reputation for being an intellectual free-spirit, individualist, and experimenter whose generosity and appetite for animated discussion in convivial surroundings all played a part in determining the somewhat soft economic base and, consequently, nomadic tendencies of the family.

So here are my aunt Elvira and cousin Joe out to make a real estate deal and buy some farmland cheap. I wasn't even conceived yet. They drove by this property, took a look, and then stopped for lunch at the local tavern down the road. The day was December 7, 1941, and the radio was on full blast at the tavern. As at least one version of the story goes, they rushed right back down the road and made a deal. Whether they got a good deal because or in spite of the events of the day, and just whatever exactly evolved to modify and dissipate those clearly etched schemes to mine the countryside for its pot of gold, I can't begin to elaborate on here, but, over time, a significant portion of this Sicilian family did migrate one step further and out onto the land. It was as if the huge bubbling metropolitan melting pot had, in its precarious teetering and swaying, hit a bump and spurted out a small dollop of its genetic stew. They bought a cow and chickens, planted their version of a Victory Garden, weathered out the war, and, during all this, I was born.

21. MOUNTAIN VIEW ROAD
looking south
Montgomery Township
April 1988

The cornfields, pastures ribboned by a meandering brook, hedge-rows following the gullies between the fields, and wooded slopes cut through by winding tractor trails leading to upper terraced fields were like a vast playground. It was like living near a wonderful park. Sheldon, Kenny, and I often sampled the young field corn in the summer, and in winter we had bicycle races on the frozen paths between the stubble of the harvested stalks. We fished in the company of clusters of grazing cows, looking always for the channels where the shallow snaking brook cut deepest into the arcing curves of the bank. By carefully following the hedgerows and avoiding the open fields, we could come up unnoticed on small herds of grazing deer, but wary crows stayed one field in advance, and the cawing alarm of their sentinels often warned away the deer.

22. TERRACELAND FARM ON
WERTSVILLE ROAD
East Amwell Township
May 1989

I remember when my dad and uncles pulled down our old collapsing barn, using long ropes attached at one end to the swaying walls and at the other to the bumper of Uncle Joe's black Buick. As the car rocked and yanked at the ropes it nearly got stuck in the mud, and then, when the wall on the near side finally did give way, the car pulled ahead barely enough to miss being hit by the crashing architecture. Later on, my uncle Bob used the barn beams in framing his house, just an acre away from where the barn had been.

23. GALLUP BARN ON MOUNTAIN VIEW ROAD
looking north
Montgomery Township
July 1990

*O*ur first cow was named Polack. My Sicilian clan had just moved out onto the countryside from a densely populated Polish neighborhood along Greenpoint Avenue in Queens, very near the Kosciusko Bridge. I am not sure if the cow was named this way in fond remembrance of the neighborhood, or as a mocking reference to a living situation they were happy to leave behind them. In any event, Polack was bred and gave birth to John Bull, who was converted to veal chops shortly thereafter.

Polack gave milk, which, in the spring, was scented and flavored with the wild garlic (*Allium vineale*) that grew everywhere in her pasture. This seasoned milk could be a challenge to drink, but the cheese my mother made from it was quite delicious.

The pasture fences weren't in great shape, so Polack had to be tethered when she grazed. Grandpa was the principal milker, and when I would go with him to watch, he would give me fresh sips of the frothy warm milk right from the pail. I remember one such occasion vividly. I was three or four years old and the early morning sun made piercing shafts of golden light throughout the barnyard, striking the cow, the froth-filled pail, my grandfather's white hair and whiskers, and the steam rising from the hot milk as it mingled with our own vaporous breath. These elements of the scene glowed intensely and held me transfixed and entranced.

24. SUNSET ROAD
looking north
Montgomery Township
February 1986

When I look at this picture I always see my grandpa in the garden. He is leaning on the handle of his spade—he always hand-spaded every inch of his garden—with his pipe in his mouth and wearing a black beret. He is looking right at me. Open fields and then a treed hillside are in the background. It is a ridge of the Watchung Mountains. Cloud patterns appear, shift, and dissolve, and the passage of time is imperceptibly gradual.

The cardoons he grew were magnificent, the centerpiece of his garden. Once, a restaurateur drove by and saw them: tall standing rows with leafy stalks bursting upward in huge fanlike clusters. He instantly bought the whole crop.

I took a picture of Grandpa when I was thirteen years old. It looks just like my description above, but I cannot find the negative or an old print. In recent years I copied a photograph for a book a friend of mine was publishing on C. G. Jung. The photograph was of Jung in his garden, leaning on a walking stick, looking exactly like my grandpa in my lost picture.

Overleaf, left
25. WERTSVILLE ROAD
looking north
East Amwell Township
March 1993

Overleaf, right
26. SERGEANTSVILLE ROAD
looking northeast
West Amwell Township
March 1993

27. FAIRVIEW ROAD
looking west
Montgomery Township
October 1985

Grandma and I took walks to the Bauer farm down the road. There she would visit with Mrs. Bauer, who wore a bonnet and sold eggs, milk, and butter from her immaculately clean front porch. The mile trek was a good outing for Grandma, but seemed a challenge for my shorter three-year-old legs.

In springtime, crossing the culvert bridge over the small pasture stream, she made me wait above while she groped down the bank and into the stream. With her skirt pulled back between her legs and tucked in at her waist, she waded in the clear flowing current and pulled up great tangled bunches of watercress. The first time this happened I was horrified. I thought she was plucking up fistfuls of snakes.

28. TOWNSHIP LINE ROAD
looking north
Montgomery Township
Detail from 1986 negative

*G*randpa's body was a rich brown color and gave off the smells of all he did and was: soil, tobacco, leather, sweat, and wine. He looked like a lanky root of some mighty weed, wrenched from deep in the earth, and, because he was always digging in the garden, he seemed to be looking for a new place to plant himself.

Whereas the earlier farmers of this New Jersey land had cultivated standard crops to feed their livestock and themselves—corn, wheat, rye, soybeans, alfalfa, berries, peaches—he added to the list eggplant, plum tomatoes, roma beans, and those glorious cardoons.

29. DEAD TREE RUN ROAD
looking east
Montgomery Township
Detail from 1986 negative

*T*he agricultural practices near my childhood homeplace were not always exemplary. There was a slaughterhouse about a mile down the road and often, in the late winter and early spring, some pretty pungent byproducts of this meat processing operation found their way out onto the soil of farm fields under the guise of fertilizer or top dressing. Tractors pulled draining tanks of dark cattle blood across the stubble-rowed cornfields, and guts, hacked knuckles, knees, and hooves were flicked here and there. The combined odors of these remnants, mingled with those of manure, urine, and the released soil scents of spring thaw, yielded an unusual and memorable bouquet.

30. CORNFIELD
Delaware Township
October 1992

We sometimes camped out in a high field, isolated from the rest of the countryside by a wall of woods. The only view was the sky. One night, equipped with telescopes, binoculars, and cameras, we photographed a UFO, and the local newspaper published our pictures in a story which included our account of the experience.

In winter, this high field was the starting point for a thrilling sled ride down the winding tractor path to the fields below. If you made all the turns on the switchbacks and kept up momentum, the whole ride was nearly a quarter of a mile long. We liked to do this ride by moonlight when the crusted snow was hard and slick.

31. CHERRY HILL ROAD
looking west
Montgomery Township
October 1985

My best early childhood outings were the fishing trips with my mother down the road at a bridge that crossed a small stream. The stream was the same meandering pasture stream that ran through all the lowest parts of our valley. The bridge, which has long since been replaced, was quaint but not historic, and there were small places to stand or sit where the abutments jutted out slightly from beneath the sides. My mom and I would also go around the sides of the bridge down to the bank in order to get closer to the deeper shaded pools underneath.

We fished with any handy coarse string, which we tied to sticks or tree branches, and opened safety pins were our hooks, which we baited with worms saved from the garden or dug with a knife right there along the bank. We caught messes of small sunfish—it must have been a spectacle of frantic activity since half the time the wriggling lively fish slipped off our barbless hooks and back into the water and we tried to grab them back with our bare hands—and we fried them in the skillet back home.

I remember a time when I stared downward both at and into the water only a few feet from my face and saw, all at once, the layers of mud, algae, and gravel of the stream bed, small fry and tadpoles flicking back and forth beneath the water's surface, striders, dragonflies, and other bugs darting in or scooting along the surface, making rippling wakes that hauntingly teased at the reflection of my own face, which was in turn surrounded by the reflected sky, trees, and clouds above and behind me. All of this was combined in one shimmering composite image, which was further enhanced and then fixed in my memory by the sounds of splashing water, our excited chatter, and the incessant insect whirr and chirping descant of a summer's day.

32. BRIDGE AT BEDENS BROOK
AND CHERRY HILL ROAD
looking north
Montgomery Township
October 1985

*I*t took many years from the time when the rumor started circulating—when I was eight or nine—that the neighboring farmland was being sold for development, to the time when I was forty years old and the deal was finally done and the building of extravagant luxury homes actually started. All those years in between comprised a season during which we all—family, friends, neighbors—went through a long but steady process of emotional preparation: accepting the inevitability of change; abandoning the hope of some reprieve or change of plan; signing off on the immutable fact that we must relinquish something we never really possessed or could control—the countryside around us. And throughout the vacuum of that suspended spell of lingering years, as unplanted fields lay fallow and began to fester with the early stages of an impossible succession back to forest, we began checking in ourselves that easy, soothing emotional release that always came when scanning the view of wide sloping fields and the treed horizon line of the cresting ridge, which ascended protectively as a wall and buttressed the dark northern sky above our valley.

33. DEAD TREE RUN ROAD
looking east
Montgomery Township
From January 1985 negative

*E*veryone knew for so long what would someday happen, and no one seemed to want this change. Yet no one took steps to try to prevent it. Years later I still wonder why. I suppose the prevailing sentiment was simply that it was someone else's land and who were we to say what they could or couldn't do with it. It didn't belong to us.

And yet, the land did belong to us, in the sense that it was a part of the lives of we who lived near it, looked out on it every day, walked over it, smelled its scents, and allowed it to etch an indelible picture of the landscape in our memories. That land wasn't just a farm, or a place to hike, sled, fish, hunt, or camp out; it was also a place where brooding thoughts and simmering hopes took shape, gnawing anguishes were allowed to dissipate, dreadful angers and hostile revenges modified, and creative visions and ardent loves were conceived. It was a place that offered to each one who lived nearby an opportunity to find, in whatever time or turn, a sense of self, and then connect it to some part of the elemental design.

34. GROVE OF TREES NEAR FIELDS
WHERE MICHELE USED TO HORSEBACKRIDE
Montgomery Township
May 1991

*E*ntering the hollow was just a swing around the bend on bikes, but a complete turn of mind. The drowsy simmering heat of the open summer roads, lined with tumbling decks of poison ivy, sumac, and honeysuckle; the spreading steaming fields of corn and soy; and the orchards, all whirring with cicadas; suddenly transformed into a cool forest-shaded road, with the silence and remoteness of a mountain retreat.

The mad artist who haunted my childhood hollow was unpredictable and potentially dangerous, or so the rumors cautioned. In his cedar-thatched chalet, he was surrounded by a lawn decorated with his wild craft creations: mini-chalets with whirlygigs of an insane gardener, which whirred and spun in the breeze. And he might come out after you.

We churned past on our bikes and loved the quickness of our fear.

35. ROCK BROOK CREEK
NEAR HOLLOW ROAD
looking east
Montgomery Township
April 1991

I had been working in the creek bed for about an hour. It was late July and a long hot spell was bearing down hard, the second-worst heat wave of the century. I chose to photograph in the creek bed mostly so I could be barefoot in the water and in the shade.

A robust, barrel-chested man came suddenly from the house across the road. He was curious about the camera, I thought, but really he wanted to tell me how this creek was part of his family and their lives. He told how he raised six sons here and this stony tumble of water was their constant playground, and how his sons' children were now also endlessly building the dams and hopping from rock to rock to the reassuring sounds of this amiable stream. Yes, they had cleared poison ivy, cut down trees, and cleared enough to build a house and make a yard, but it was the creek that made it all.

36. ROCK BROOK CREEK
NEAR HOLLOW ROAD
looking north
Montgomery Township
July 1988

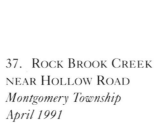

37. ROCK BROOK CREEK
NEAR HOLLOW ROAD
Montgomery Township
April 1991

38, 39, 40. Struggle in the Sourlands
Hillsborough Township
April 1992

Opposite
41. DEVIL'S HALF ACRE
Sourland Mountain Preserve
Hillsborough Township
May 1989

42. ROARING ROCKS
Sourland Mountain Preserve
Montgomery Township
May 1989

*T*he Millstone River flood plain presents a medley of life forms, progressing from aquatic to arboreal, with open stretches of tufted grasslands in between, back and forth, stretching for miles.

Close to the stream are deep-cut banks, topped with flood-bent grass and trees leaning crazily out over the muddy cleavage, their lower branches bearded with caught flotsam, lower trunks all sepia in sunlight, coated with mud slips by the swift spring flows.

Farther out from the channel way, across open grassy spaces, are jungles of smaller trees laced with vines, briars, and poison ivy; everything mixed in a collective tangle of intertwined limbs. Here all life is linked in a single matted mass, and there is a great feeling of somber movement, like witnessing a grave passion play as it follows through an eternally slow progress, through stations of sacrifice and pain, redemption and rebirth.

43. MILLSTONE RIVER
NEAR GRIGGSTOWN
looking east
Montgomery Township
April 1990

44. MILLSTONE RIVER FLOOD
PLAIN NEAR RIVER ROAD
looking east
Montgomery Township
April 1990

45. MILLSTONE RIVER
NEAR RIVER ROAD
looking north
Montgomery Township
April 1988

46. VIRTUAL TREESCAPE
Delaware and Raritan Canal
between Griggstown and Rocky Hill
Franklin Township
Spring 1992

*T*he Millstone River flows in varying proximity to the Delaware and Raritan Canal, sometimes practically touching the edges of the towpath, and in other places meandering widely separate with large areas of woods and grassy flood plain between. It is in these marshy junglelike areas between Griggstown and Millstone that the phantom cows reside.

It is said that these cows escaped from their pasture some ten or twelve years ago, and no one has ever been able to recapture them. Rare sightings are reported from time to time, but otherwise they remain invisible and unknown. It was my plan, when working on a series of night scenes, to explore this area with bright halogen beams and find them, these unfettered and elusive renegades. Surprise them and take their picture. But I somehow never got around to it.

47. VIRTUAL TREESCAPE
Delaware and Raritan Canal
between Griggstown and Rocky Hill
Franklin Township
Spring 1992

48, 49. VIRTUAL TREESCAPES
Delaware and Raritan Canal
between Griggstown and Rocky Hill
Franklin Township
Spring 1992

50. VIRTUAL TREESCAPE
Delaware and Raritan Canal between Griggstown and Rocky Hill
Franklin Township
Spring 1992

Opposite
51. SYCAMORE ALONG STONY BROOK
Hopewell Township
March 1993

52, 53. STONY BROOK
looking south
Hopewell Township
March 1993

54. MILLSTONE RIVER
NEAR GRIGGSTOWN
looking west
Montgomery Township
January 1989

55. BEDENS BROOK AT GREAT ROAD
looking east
Montgomery Township
January 1989

56. BEDENS BROOK
NEAR RIVER ROAD
looking east
Montgomery Township
January 1989

57. BEDENS BROOK
AT OPOSSUM ROAD
looking southwest
Montgomery Township
January 1989

Opposite
58. BEDENS BROOK NEAR RIVER ROAD
looking south
Montgomery Township
January 1989

59. BEDENS BROOK NEAR ROUTE 206
looking southwest
Montgomery Township
January 1989

60. GREAT ROAD AT BLAWENBURG
looking north
Montgomery Township
October 1985

When there was a house next to the barn, between the barn and the road, before the road had to be widened and improved, a solitary man lived there. A hermit. Some said his name was Voorhees and that he never spoke to anyone. Nevertheless, he always nodded when I rode by on my bicycle. Usually he was in the vegetable garden, which was all beans and chard. His staple foods, I assumed. Dressed in ancient green fatigues, he blended with his crops, and his complexion imitated the weathered, unpainted tones of his shingled house, the barn, and the rambling rails of wooden fence.

He kept everything in artful order. Each broken board of siding or shingle was carefully repositioned in its original place; each fallen rail of fence propped, wedged, or tied back up; the lawn carefully trimmed; and occasional vines were neatly trailed along a border or rail.

But the most stunning thing of all was the opposite side of the road, where scruffy, gnarled trees lined the unruly edge. Carefully arranged in lavish sunburst designs around the base of each tree were all the roadside leavings: Schmidts, Miller, Bud, Majorska, Southern Comfort, Seagrams, Thunderbird, Ripple. The glistening found art of the countryside composed like jewels. Country brooches here and there and necklaces for each sorry little tree.

The house is gone, the artist departed, the road is improved, the barn will go next, and now I ride in another direction.

61. PROVINCE LINE ROAD
looking north
Montgomery Township
April 1990

62. PROVINCE LINE ROAD
looking north
Montgomery Township
Detail from October 1985 negative

63. PROVINCE LINE ROAD
looking north
Montgomery Township
October 1985

64. PROVINCE LINE ROAD
looking north
Montgomery Township
Detail from October 1985 negative

65. GALLUP FARM
looking east
Blawenburg
August 1988

*H*ere is a little minestrone or provincial stew. A small collection of remembered images which, like food from the garden, must be harvested when ripe and served right up:

Mr. Voorhees is outside his house, in the garden that is his front lawn, stooped over among the string beans. Swiss chard is to his left. Just a glimpse as I cycle by.

Clouds move slowly over a double row of trees near Planters Row. This twin hedgerow was meant to be a break to the prevailing northwesterly wind, to keep it from sweeping away the soil in a time when the land was actually cultivated. Now I can see the clouds clearly, but the trees are eclipsed by huge houses. The many peaks of roofs and dormers, several tall chimneys, picket fence posts and flagpoles, all parts of these imposing domiciles, are trying to poke away the clouds.

There is a great blue heron nesting in the Bedens Brook, but I won't say where.

I am coming swiftly down Grandview Hill, riding in a bicycle race. It is late October, windy and cold. It is the club's end-of-the-season championship race. We have crested the bump at the top and are screaming down the steep straight when I notice, off to the side in the field, running diagonal to our course as if to intercept us, with furious bounds spanning immense stretches, a jackrabbit. He has the speed, massive hindquarters with thighs of a sprinter, but he lacks the staying power. Finally, he just stops and sits, right in the middle of the field. We ride on and I never see him, or another, again.

66. BEDENS BROOK ROAD
looking north
Montgomery Township
October 1985

The Canada geese are beginning their annual ritual of grouping and regrouping in the fields where the corn has just been harvested. Small flocks come and go throughout the day and night, eventually settling in with the increasingly larger clan. Very close to our village.

They are choosing leaders, I think. Each smaller group is sending forth its captains to meet in the honking debate; deciding how to form the larger companies, then squadrons and platoons. Ultimately they will choose a general to be in overall command. Participating crows, acting as sentinels and scouts, form around the periphery where they conduct conferences of their own.

Furtively under cover with binoculars and cameras, I watch their movements and wonder: Will they migrate this year, or are they plotting some big surprise?

Perhaps they will be joined by prancing packs of vicious wolves and rowdy stumbling bears who will come spewing down from the hillsides. Joined together, a nasty bunch like that could serve us our deserts.

67. BLAWENBURG
looking north
Montgomery Township
Detail from February 1986 negative

Mr. Young, whose farmhouse this was, died a few years after I took this picture. He was in his nineties.

I knew this fact only vaguely, until one day it all came seriously home to me as I drove by and saw the auction. Cars were all up and down the road, filling up on the ebbing contents of the house. By late afternoon they had driven away with just about everything but the molding, banisters, and plumbing.

Some weeks later I heard rumors that the house was being stripped of even these remaining features.

I never saw Mr. Young or the inside of his house, before or after it was stripped, nor was I around the week the bulldozers finished off the job. The remains of the house were probably trucked off to a landfill, which is ironic since this very property was one of several sites being considered by officials as a possible landfill, even when Mr. Young was still living there.

68. GRAND VIEW ROAD
looking north
Montgomery Township
Detail from 1985 negative

*E*ach year it seems as though the sea birds appear earlier in these inland farm fields. It is now mid-February and I have noticed them for over a week already. Their outlines in the sky make a distinct contrast—their angular swept-back wing and pointed-tip design—to the more familiar shapes of the crows, starlings, pigeons, doves, hawks, and vultures one usually sees throughout the winter. With the ground now frozen hard and patched with ice and crusted snow, they must be feeding mostly on the top dressing of stable cleanings being spread over the fields in preparation for the spring plowing. But when the thaw is final and that plowing begins, they will feast in swooping hordes, lining the freshly turned furrows only feet behind the passing plows, gorging themselves on endless quantities of unearthed grubs, beetles, worms, spider eggs, and insect larva to the point where they cannot even fly.

69. BEDENS BROOK ROAD
looking south
Montgomery Township
February 1986

When something is done to a piece of land such as paving a driveway, roadway, parking lot; or putting in curbs, sidewalks, culverts, bridges; or erecting light poles, signs, houses, garages, gas stations, stores; these are all called improvements to the land.

When plans for the subdivision and development of large tracts of land are made, many improvements are involved and much governmental attention and review are necessary.

In the course of subdivision review, preliminary approvals must come first, allowing many of the infrastructure improvements to commence; and when the subdivision plans are finally approved, the subdivision is called perfected.

Undeveloped land, or land in the natural state, is called unimproved land, and it is sometimes referred to as raw land. (Incidentally, if parts of this raw land are restricted from improvements by the imposition of a conservation easement or a deed restriction, it is said that the land has been damaged.)

Perhaps we could say that land which has received preliminary approval is no longer raw, but cooked.

And then, perhaps we could say that when land has received final approval for subdivision and development, and the subdivision is perfected, that the land is done.

And then again, perhaps, if all the parcels of raw land in a region are so perfected and approved, to the maximum allowable density permitted by local zoning, we could proclaim the land well done.

70. BEDENS BROOK AT GREAT ROAD
looking west
Montgomery Township
Detail from September 1985 negative

*M*emory invades thought, cutting through like the flashes of a summer evening storm, suddenly illuminating details here and there. The images burn deep into my eye and then, in quick gradient, fade back, like sleep, into the dark surround.

71. NIGHT IMAGES
Blawenburg
Montgomery Township
New Year's Eve 1990

*M*ost of what is in these night pictures is selected from memory and "painted" in or rendered with moving spotlights or selectively aimed flashes of a strobe.

In a similar vein, I have always thought that dreaming is a semiconscious effort to illuminate, isolate, and focus on subjects of concern. My dreams are often attempts to revisit unresolved problems or some internal debate, or to dwell selectively on a thing or idea with which I am passionately involved.

Accordingly, I see the photographic process in these night pictures as being like dreaming. It is also like painting or drawing or writing poetry in that it is a process where I am selectively adding details. The rhythmic element of poetry registers in the blurred or compound images made by moving water, clouds, leaves, grass, or by the punctuation of bursts of the strobe, or the bouncing lines made by my walking through the scene with a flashlight, or the streaks of car lights as they drive by.

72. NIGHT IMAGES
Rock Brook Creek near
Hollow Road
Montgomery Township
April 1992

We always had chickens when I was young. My dad said we had as many as two hundred laying hens at a time. This was during the latter part of World War II and the years immediately following. He sold eggs at the factory where he worked. Sometimes he took in surplus vegetables from the garden—our Victory Garden.

The printing plant where he worked had been converted to the making of huge antiaircraft guns to shoot down Nazi rockets and planes. But by the time I was three years old, the big war was over.

I still had my own personal war to fight in the barnyard. I used to love to collect the eggs, often sliding my hands under warm hens still setting, who clucked loudly in protest. Sometimes I would take an especially warm egg and bang it on a protruding nail and suck out the warm inside. But the policing roosters, on guard duty, were often on to my game, and they would come furiously flapping at me, trapping me in the corner of the pen, jumping and kicking at me in a mad, blitzing frenzy. Then I had to tuck in and hold off until adults would come running, shoo away the frantic fowl and free me. Once, because he was there for me just at the right time, my dad caught an attacking rooster in the midst of its kamikaze dive at me. His arm shot out and caught the rocketing rooster in mid-flight and he wrung its neck on the spot.

73. NIGHT IMAGES
Barnyard in Blawenburg
Montgomery Township
May 1992

*S*lowly walking in the darkened stream bed, slipping only slightly on the surface of the algae-coated rock below the surface of the warm July water, I try to remember when, as a boy, I waded barefoot in deeply silted pasture streams and tried to scramble up high curving walls of mud on cutaway banks, grasping for the cresting ledges of grassy overhang, trying to avoid stepping on snakes and turtles, looking for the best spot to catch a fish—some deep little shaded pool near an exposed tree root.

Now, in near total darkness, standing securely booted on the rock ledge that is this firmer stream bed, I welcome, with some puzzlement and apprehension, the visits of curiously aggressive bullfrogs, small trout who jump furiously at the moths and mosquitoes my lights attract to the water's surface, and the dreamy snakes of summer who swim slowly by and seem to see or care about nothing at all.

74. NIGHT IMAGES
Bedens Brook near
Great Road
Montgomery Township
July 1992

*T*hese night images are elusive and they evolve over time. Each picture emerges from within as an impression left by memory. I have been to these places, or places like them, many times before. When I return at night, the composition is already framed in my mind's eye, but I must now find it with the spotlight. It is necessary to reach out across the darkness to that place where, seemingly detached from the ground I stand on, the image floats, framed on all sides by darkness.

Sometimes what I imagined isn't there at all, or there is something completely different and unexpected. A surprise.

75. NIGHT IMAGES
Moon over cornfield
Blawenburg
Montgomery Township
July 1992

76. NIGHT IMAGES
Rock Brook Creek
near Burnt Hill Road
Montgomery Township
July 1992

77. NIGHT IMAGES
Rock Brook Creek
near Burnt Hill Road
Montgomery Township
July 1992

78. NIGHT IMAGES
Barnyard in Blawenburg
Montgomery Township
May 1992

Opposite
79. NIGHT IMAGES
Forest canopy near
Rock Brook Creek
Montgomery Township
April 1992

Natives

Over the Bedens Brook arcing hawks turn in wide circles,
like their brethren in our western skies,
the eagles.

The curves of their prayerfully silent soar
conjure shapes which caress, imitate, and hold
the earth.

Their gesturing wingtips whisper in a mysterious way,
signing in an ancient language, asking a response
from us.

I watch and wonder if some of us will read the sign,
answer with a chant, dance and join
the tribe.

80. BEDENS BROOK NEAR GREAT ROAD
looking west
Montgomery Township
April 1988

*F*or the central New Jersey region, sprawling expanses of residential and commercial development have emerged as the new agriculture: a kind of one-time cash-crop farming where the yield is bushels of dollars, often harvested primarily by those who don't even reside or operate their development businesses within the region. Remaining unharvested in the soil as a permanently abiding residue are the roots of this crop: vast deposits of many tons of concrete; insinuated veins of miles of pipe, steel, and wire; boundless glacial sheets of asphalt; lakes and reservoirs of pesticides, preservatives, petrochemicals, paints, and dyes; and ever-thickening layers of landfill bog which are the repositories of disposable hopes and plastic dreams. What form of natural process and compression, combined with what geologic measurement of time, can make a region like this organically fertile again, and what crops will then emerge?

81. ALONG BEDENS BROOK
NEAR WASHINGTON WELL FARM
Montgomery Township
April 1988

*T*his image was made late in the day. It is a very exciting but vexing time to be photographing. The light is most dramatic, yet unpredictably changeable. There are elaborate patterns created by lengthening shadows, strong glowing backlight effects, and intensely deep hues appear in portions of clear sky opposite the setting sun, which often forcefully accent traversing clouds. But one must work quickly and precisely as these conditions evolve rapidly, culminating in a brief span of time, and then they quickly fade.

Occasionally, I am caught off guard, speeding frantically back and forth in my truck on roads traveled earlier in the day, trying to find those spots I noted might yield good lighting later on, trying to remember just where it was I meant to be and knowing this is the last chance before I lose all good light.

Fortunately, I got in position just in time for this view of a farm. The shadow of me, atop the elevated platform with the view camera, appears in the right foreground of the picture near the For Sale sign. It was at the point when I was all set up and actually making exposures that the farmer and his helper pulled up in the pickup truck:

"Hello," I called down in greeting. I always make a friendly overture in situations like this. Sometimes there is a 12-gauge shotgun or a rifle in the truck and a scowl on the face. "Is this your farm?"

"Yep. You want to buy it?" He was leaning out of the driver-side window, twisting his neck up and squinting at me. He was almost smiling and I sensed a friend.

"No. I wish I could, but I can't. Someone will soon, though. Looks like you got missed this last round in the development boom." He nodded. "But you will get a chance next round. Your farm is on a major east-west route here."

"I hope so. I can't hold out too much longer." And he launched himself into a major recitation, in which he referred to things I have heard so many times before from other farmers in this region who have all, because of rising land values, been under economic pressure to relinquish their land for development. He talked about how he, as well as 65 percent of all farm owners in the state, is over sixty years old, and how their children can't or won't carry on the farm; how the market makes it impossible to earn a profit growing the traditional feed crops and cattle; how the state farmland preservation program pays too little and cannot give adequate priority to this area of the state with its disproportionately higher land values; and how impossible it is getting for him to continue rising before 4:00 A.M. and working until 8:00 or sometimes 10:00 each night, seven days a week, at his age.

As we talked, I continued making exposures and tried to reassure him that the next building boom would be just around the corner. Finally, he drove back up the road to the house. The sun was soon eclipsed by the horizon behind me, and the envelope of advancing shadow finally enshrouded the earthly view and only the sky remained bright.

82. ROSEMONT–RINGOES ROAD
looking east
Delaware Township
October 1992

83. AMWELL RIDGE FARM
looking southwest
East Amwell Township
October 1992

84. AMWELL RIDGE FARM
Rocktown Road
looking north
East Amwell Township
October 1992

I could have used a wider-angle lens when photographing this barn scene and then, visible in the picture just down the road to the right, would have been a surveyor and his van. This engineer, at work with his transit and clipboard with plans, was in position when I arrived sometime after 10:00 A.M. By the time I had finished taking the picture, a backhoe and dozer had arrived and started digging. By the end of the day, passing back this way just before sunset, I could see that the excavation for the foundation of the house was complete. There is no doubt in my mind that the basement was poured and the frame erected before I even got to develop my negative.

85. WERTSVILLE ROAD
looking northeast
East Amwell Township
October 1992

86. WERTSVILLE ROAD
looking northeast
East Amwell Township
October 1992

Opposite
87. SANDBROOK HEADQUARTERS
ROAD
looking east
Delaware Township
October 1992

O ur country roadsides contain an insane variety of plants and creatures.

They present sumac, honeysuckle, poison ivy, wild strawberry, chicory, thistle, milkweed, nightshade, Queen Anne's lace, snapdragon, ragweed, grape, tiger lily, cattail, bristlegrass, rushes, nettle, smartweed, pokeweed, buttercup, shepherd's-purse, winter cress, verbena, horehound, field morning glory, sorrel, cockle, Indian tobacco, quackgrass, goldenrod, aster, fleabane, heal-all, horseweed, black-eyed Susan, joe-pye weed, yarrow, chamomile, field daisy, and much more.

In tandem with these myriad plant species, these roadside borders also support or protect snakes, turtles, rabbits, groundhogs, pheasants, foxes, nesting birds, bees, butterflies, rats, mice, voles, praying mantises, ladybugs, beetles, spiders, fireflies, katydids, crickets, and feral cats, along with those domestic cats who are allowed to be part-time hunters.

Townships and counties maintain these roadsides in order to ensure proper drainage and keep sightlines clear. A major part of this maintenance is the periodic summer mowing along the right of way. These mowings keep this wild profusion of plant and animal life in constant disarray and in a fierce struggle for dominance. It is all lots of work for both wildlife and humans.

As we develop the rural land, we reconstruct these frontages with improved and widened roadways, which meet perfectly matched curbs, along which run cement sidewalks. Along the sidewalks, and consistent with the usually compulsively maintained lawns of new homes, we plant a grass which is singular in type and appearance, easily mowed, and always kept at uniform height. Neat, easy to maintain, and much less work for all concerned.

88. HOLLOW ROAD
looking west
Montgomery Township
July 1990

89. GREAT ROAD NEAR BLAWENBURG
looking east
Montgomery Township
July 1990

90. HOLLOW ROAD
looking east
Montgomery Township
July 1990

91. ROUTE 518 NEAR
BURNT HILL ROAD
looking west
Montgomery Township
May 1991

92. SKILLMAN ROAD
looking south
Montgomery Township
May 1991

Glossary

Preliminary approvals, Final approvals,
   and all that's in between.
Major, Minor   subdivision,
      with or without
            professional review.
Plats with scales
               and fine details—
                     the caliper of trees.
Matchlines when it's all too big and one page isn't enough to showitall.
Specifications to the nth degree
            and of course
               themaximumallowabledensity.

And each new lot
which does conform,
Minimum setbacks,
All perks confirm,
The final touch,
That cozy little
      safe closure,

                  the building
                  envelope

Then there are, in pious tones,
               the references, the deferences,
                                 to those
(Sensitive areas)   *ENVIRONMENTAL IMPACT STATEMENT!*
You have your
         steep
               slopes,
wetlands,
      floodplains,
            faults.
Not our fault—   *—Not your fault.*
               they are like children with defects
Accidental freaks of nature,
               obligingly given attention by some,
                     spoken of with gravity and much concern,
But ultimately segregated out, given up,
                     as deformed children are;
      Dedicated
            to the foster care of the state.

93. FERNS ALONG BROOKVILLE
HOLLOW ROAD
Delaware Township
October 1992

94. ROUTE 601 NEAR BLAWENBURG
looking east
Montgomery Township
August 1988

About the Author

Clem Fiori is a free-lance photographer whose work has been exhibited and published widely. He is an appointed municipal official, and chair of an Open Space Committee, in Montgomery Township, New Jersey.